Separation of Church & State

WHAT THE FOUNDERS MEANT

David Barton

5/27/2010

Aledo, Texas
www.wallbuilders.com

Separation of Church and State: What the Founders Meant
Copyright © 2007 David Barton
1st Edition, 3nd Printing, 2009

Additional materials available from:
WallBuilders
P. O. Box 397
Aledo, TX 76008
(817) 441-6044
www.wallbuilders.com

Cover Photo:
Interior of National Cathedral – Washington, DC

Cover Design:
Jeremiah Pent
Lincoln-Jackson
838 Walden Dr
Franklin TN 37064

Library of Congress Cataloging-in-Publication Data
342.029
Barton, David
Separation of Church and State: What the Founders Meant.
Aledo, TX: WallBuilder Press
16 p.; 21 cm.
Endnotes included.
A transcript of the video and audio by the title *Foundations of American Government*.
ISBN-10: 1-932225-41-2
ISBN-13: 978-1-932225-41-9
B29f
1. Church and state – U. S.   2. Religion and politics   3. U. S. – Constitutional history   I. Title

Printed in the United States of America

Separation of Church & State
What the Founders Meant

In recent years, right-thinking Americans have been repeatedly shocked and perplexed by unimaginable random acts of violence. The numbers of mass shootings at schools, cafeterias, subways, postal facilities, and churches, and bombings at government and private office buildings have been almost mind-boggling. And who would have imagined that an unpopular court decision in California and a victorious basketball game in Illinois would each cause widespread rioting and looting with human casualties and massive property destruction?

Such events not only offend the sensibilities of normal citizens but they also serve as reminders of the unhappy fact that far too many among us no longer possess the time-honored qualities of civility and decency – far too many lack the internal restraints necessary to prevent explosive violent outbursts. Perhaps such tragic events may yet result in lasting good if they cause us to re-embrace the teachings and public policies that once produced the individual character and virtues necessary for a genuinely civilized society.

Significantly, numerous Founding Fathers and early statesmen asserted that religious faith was the most important source of those civil virtues. Among those holding this view were DECLARATION SIGNERS John Hancock, [1] John Adams, [2] Benjamin Rush, [3] Thomas Jefferson, [4] Robert Treat Paine, [5] Charles Carroll, [6] John Witherspoon, [7] etc.; CONSTITUTION SIGNERS George Washington, [8] Benjamin Franklin, [9] James McHenry, [10] Abraham Baldwin, [11] Gouverneur Morris, [12] William Paterson, [13] etc.; FAMOUS STATESMEN Patrick Henry, [14] Noah Webster, [15] John Quincy Adams, [16] Daniel Webster, [17] etc.; and many, many others.

And religious faith not only produced America's most important civil virtues but it was also a primary reason for the founding of America. As U. S. Supreme Court Chief Justice John Marshall affirmed:

One great object of the colonial charters was avowedly the propagation of the Christian faith. [18]

The same religious faith that founded America also guided her through her establishment as an independent nation. As John Adams acknowledged:

The general principles on which the fathers achieved independence were. . . . the general principles of Christianity. [19]

Leader after leader, from generation to generation, from the Framers to contemporary statesmen, reaffirmed this fact – such as when President Harry Truman openly avowed:

In this great country of ours has been demonstrated the fundamental unity of Christianity and democracy. [20]

The principles of faith were incorporated into our governing documents from the very beginning, and the positive results have been obvious. As French observer Alexis de Tocqueville reported in his famous work *Democracy in America*:

[T]here is no country in the whole world in which the Christian religion retains a greater influence over the souls of men than in America – and there can be no greater proof of its utility, and of its conformity to human nature, than that its influence is most powerfully felt over the most enlightened and free nation of the earth. [21]

America truly has been blessed with a unique form of government. Its governing documents (the Declaration of Independence, the Constitution, and the Bill of Rights) have brought this nation to a position unrivaled by any other over the past two centuries, and religious principles were a powerful influence in shaping each of those documents.

Yet, notwithstanding the positive influence of religious faith in forming America's distinctive culture, it seems that the greatest influence today in sculpting the faith and values of American culture is the extraconstitutional phrase "separation of church and state." Significantly, that now-popular phrase is found in none of our governing documents, despite the widespread modern belief to the contrary.

A conversation I once had with a U. S. Congressman (who is also an accomplished attorney) illustrates how deeply this non-constitutional phrase has been infused in our constitutional thinking. As we were discussing the importance of basic religious values and teachings to public behavior and society in general, he lamented, "We know these values are important; it's unfortunate that we can't do anything to promote them."

Surprised, I queried, "Why not?"

He replied, "We just can't."

I persisted, "Why not?"

He answered, "Because of 'separation of church and state.'"

I responded, "'Separation of church and state'? What about it?"

He replied, "It's in the Constitution – the Constitution won't permit us to have religious values in public arenas."

I returned, "That phrase is not in the Constitution!"

Forcefully he countered, "Yes it is!"

"No it's not."

"Yes it is."

We went back and forth. I finally gave him a copy of the Constitution and asked, "Would you please find that phrase for me?"

He replied triumphantly, "I'd be happy to!" He immediately turned to the First Amendment, read it – and became very embarrassed. He said, "I can't believe this! In law school they always taught us that's what the First Amendment said!"

Amazed, I asked, "You've never read the Constitution for yourself?"

He replied, "We were never required to read it in law school!"

This conversation illustrates a common misconception. Many citizens believe that the phrase "separation of church and state" is language found in our governing documents; it is not. Concerning religion, the Constitution (specifically, the First Amendment to the Constitution) states only that "Congress shall make no law respecting an establishment of religion or prohibiting the free exercise thereof." The words "separation," "church," or "state" are not found in the First Amendment, the Constitution, or in any other official founding document.

Yet, even after learning that the phrase is not part of the Constitution, many citizens nevertheless persist: "Well, even though the words aren't there, isn't that what the First Amendment really means? Wasn't that the intent of those who framed that Amendment?" The answer to that question is, "No; that was not their intent" – at least not in the way that we have come to know separation of church and state today.

What evidence proves this? The Founders' own writings as well as the official documents surrounding the framing of the First Amendment – documents such as the *Congressional Record*.

The *Congressional Record* (required by the Constitution in Art. 1, Sec. 5, ¶ 3) contains all the official words and acts that occur in congressional chambers. Those records therefore include the discussion of the ninety Founders in the first federal Congress who, from June 8 to September 25, 1789, framed the First Amendment. [22] In those lengthy discussions that spanned months, the Founders repeatedly explained that they were seeking to prevent what they had experienced under Great Britain: the legal establishment by the national government of a single religious denomination in exclusion of all others (whether Catholic, Anglican, or any other). Very simply, their oft-repeated intent was that Congress could not officially establish any one denomination in America; or, in the wording proposed by James Madison, "nor shall any *national* religion be established." [23]

(Significantly, the word "religion" in the Founders' First Amendment discussions was often used interchangeably with the word "denomination." For example, the original version of the First Amendment introduced in the Senate on September 3, 1789, stated, "Congress shall not make any law establishing any religious *denomination*." The second version stated, "Congress shall make no law establishing any particular *denomination*." The third version was very similar, declaring, "Congress shall make no law establishing any particular denomination in preference to another." The final version passed on that day declared, "Congress shall make no law establishing religion or prohibiting the free exercise thereof." [24] Clearly, the word "religion" had been used interchangeably with "denomination" throughout their discussions, and this is why the First Amendment prohibited the national government from establishing any single "religion," or denomination.)

When the First Amendment was finally approved, it contained two separate clauses on religion, each with an independent scope of action. The first clause (called the Establishment Clause) prohibited the federal government from establishing a single national denomination; the second clause (called the Free Exercise Clause) prohibited the federal government from interfering with the people's public religious expressions and acknowledgments. Significantly, both clauses restricted the actions of the federal government; neither restricted the actions of citizens. Very simply, the Founding Fathers did not want a single federal denomination to rule America ("Congress shall make no law respecting the establishment of religion . . ."), but they did expect basic Biblical principles and values to be present throughout public life and society (". . . nor prohibiting the free exercise thereof").

Significantly, for over a century-and-a-half after the First Amendment was ratified, this was the **_only_** manner in which it was interpreted. Unfortunately, in recent decades activist courts have dramatically redefined the word "religion" in the First Amendment, giving it a definition found in **_no_** dictionary (except the Court's own privately-written one). The result is that the First Amendment is now used to **_prohibit_** the very religious activities that the Founders themselves once **_encouraged_** under that same Amendment.

One clear example of this is provided by Fisher Ames, the Founding Father who offered the final wording for the House version of the First Amendment. [25] Ames, like so many other Framers, was committed to maintaining sound education in America. In his watchfulness over education, he noticed that many new children's books, filled with character fables and moral lessons, were being introduced into the classroom. Ames did not object to the content of these new books, but he was alarmed that an unintended consequence would be that students would have less time to spend on the Bible. He therefore publicly urged:

> Why then, if these [new] books for children must be retained – as they will be – should not the Bible regain the place it once held as a school book? [26]

Ames further noted that the Bible was the principal source of sound morals in America and therefore must never be separated from the classroom. [27]

Clearly, the use of the Bible in public school classrooms did not violate Fisher Ames' view of the First Amendment – and he was one of the Framers most responsible for the wording of that Amendment. Ironically, the Amendment he helped write now prohibits the very activities he once encouraged under that same Amendment.

Dr. Benjamin Rush provides another such example. Rush signed the Declaration of Independence, ratified the Constitution, and served in the presidential administrations of John Adams, Thomas Jefferson, and James Madison. He was also one of America's leading educators, helping found five schools and universities, three of which still exist today. In fact, he was the first Founder to call for free public schools under the Constitution, [28] for which he may properly be titled "The Father of the Public Schools under the Constitution."

In a famous 1791 educational policy paper, Rush offered numerous reasons why the Bible should never be taken out of American schools. He even warned:

> In contemplating the political institutions of the United States, [if we remove the Bible from schools] I lament that we waste so much time and money in punishing crimes and take so little pains to prevent them. [29]

Rush knew that if religious teachings were excluded from education, widespread misbehavior would result, and the increase in crime would become a national problem. Yet today the First Amendment now prohibits what it once protected: the inclusion of religious principles in public education.

Noah Webster provides additional corroboration of the Founders' views on this subject. Webster today is primarily known only as an educator (his impact on education was so profound that he has been titled the "Schoolmaster to America"), yet he was also a Founding Father, serving as a soldier during the Revolution and a legislator and judge afterwards. He was one of the first Founders to call for the Constitutional Convention and was personally responsible for specific wording in the Constitution. In a textbook he authored for public schools, Webster told students:

> All the miseries and evils which men suffer from vice, crime, ambition, injustice, oppression, slavery, and war, proceed from their despising or neglecting the precepts contained in the Bible. [30]

Very simply, the Founders understood the numerous societal benefits produced by Biblical precepts and values and had no intention of expunging those principles from the public square. They even believed that American government would not function properly if separated from religious principles. As John Adams explained:

> [W]e have no government armed with power capable of contending with human passions unbridled by morality and religion. . . . Our Constitution was made *only* for a moral and religious people. It is wholly inadequate to the government of any other. [31] (emphasis added)

Adams was one of only two Founders to sign the Bill of Rights (and thus the First Amendment), and as a constitutional expert, he forcefully pronounced that our Constitution would not function properly if separated from religious values and standards. Yet, contemporary courts now use the document that bears his signature to prohibit what he encouraged under that same document.

Significantly, subsequent generations retained the Framers' beliefs about the importance of Biblical principles in maintaining a civilized society. For example, Robert Winthrop, a Speaker of the U. S. House of Representatives in the 1840s, repeated what he had learned from the Framers, explaining:

> Men, in a word, must necessarily be controlled either by a power within them or by a power without them, either by the Word of God or by the strong arm of man, either by the Bible or by the bayonet. [32]

(There are similar authoritative declarations from numerous other Framers and early statesmen.)

Given the Founders' unequivocal position on the necessity of including religious principles and expressions throughout the public arena, is it reasonable to believe that they would create an Amendment whose alleged purpose was to prohibit what they so cherished and advocated? Certainly not! To the contrary, not only did the Founders never intend that the First Amendment be a vehicle to separate religious principles from public affairs but they believed that through its Free Exercise clause they had protected these principles and kept them in the public square.

One of the clearest affirmations of the Framer's commitment to retaining religious principles in official arenas came from President George Washington, who presided over the formation of both the Constitution and the Bill of Rights. In his famous "Farewell Address," [†] Washington reminded Americans that religious teachings and values must *never* be removed from politics and public policy, declaring:

> Of all the dispositions and habits which lead to *political* prosperity, religion and morality are ***indispensable*** [insepa-

---

† For generations, students were taught that Washington's "Farewell Address" was the most significant political speech ever delivered by an American President. That address was regularly printed as a separate school textbook and many states required that students be tested over the content of that Address. Unfortunately, Washington's Address is virtually unknown today and has not been seen in its entirety in most history textbooks for nearly five decades (the same period of time, incidentally, in which the secular "separation" doctrine has been so aggressively advanced). Why has this great Address now disappeared? Perhaps because of Washington's unequivocal and overt endorsement of religion in the public arena.

rable] supports. In vain would that man claim the tribute of patriotism, who should labor to subvert these great pillars of human happiness – these firmest props of the duties of men and citizens. The mere politician, equally with the pious man, ought to respect and to cherish them. [33] (emphasis added)

Notice that Washington even asserted that if anyone tried to separate religion and morality from public life and policy, he could not be called a patriot! Washington was not finished, however; he next warned Americans to reject the proposition that morality could be preserved apart from religion:

[L]et us with caution indulge the supposition that morality can be maintained without religion. Whatever may be conceded to the influence of refined education ... reason and experience both forbid us to expect that national morality can prevail in exclusion of religious principle. [34]

Washington, understanding that religion was the basis of morality and that there was no secure basis for a free government apart from religion, therefore insightfully queried:

Let it simply be asked, Where is the security for property, for reputation, for life, if the sense of religious obligation desert the oaths which are the instruments of investigation in courts of justice? [35]

Washington warned that if religious principles were separated from public institutions such as our courts of justice, then citizens would no longer have a secure basis for property, life, or freedom.

Clearly, the writings not only of George Washington but also of John Adams, Benjamin Rush, Fisher Ames, John Marshall, Noah Webster, James Madison, and many other prominent Founders make clear that they did **_not_** embrace the secular "separation" philosophy imposed on America today, and supposedly imposed under the authority of the Constitution they wrote.

Yet, if the phrase "separation of church and state" appears in no official founding document, then what is the source of that phrase? And how did it become so closely associated with the First Amendment?

On October 7, 1801, the Danbury Baptist Association of Danbury, Connecticut, sent a letter to President Thomas Jefferson expressing their concern that protection for religion had been written into the laws and constitutions. Believing strongly that freedom of religion was an inalienable right given by God, the fact that it appeared in civil documents suggested that the government viewed it as a government-granted rather than a God-granted right. Apprehensive that the government might someday wrongly believe that it did have the power to regulate public religious activities, the Danbury Baptists communicated their anxiety to President Jefferson. [36]

On January 1, 1802, Jefferson responded to their letter. He understood their concerns and agreed with them that man accounted only to God and not to government for his faith and religious practice. Jefferson emphasized to the Danbury Baptists that none of man's natural (i.e., inalienable) rights – including the right to exercise one's faith publicly – would ever place him in a situation where the government would interfere with his religious expressions. [37] He assured them that because of the wall of separation, they need not fear government interference with religious expressions:

> Believing with you that religion is a matter which lies solely between man and his God, . . . I contemplate with sovereign reverence that act of the whole American people which declared that their legislature should "make no law respecting an establishment of religion or prohibiting the free exercise thereof," thus building a wall of separation between Church and State. [38]

In his letter, Jefferson made clear that the "wall of separation" was erected not to limit public religious expressions but rather to provide security against governmental interference with those expressions, whether private or public. (On numerous other occasions, Jefferson repeatedly affirmed that the sole purpose of the First Amendment was to ensure that the federal government could not interfere with public religious expressions. [39])

Later courts occasionally cited Jefferson's "separation" letter in their rulings. For example, in the 1878 case *Reynolds v. United States*, the Supreme Court quoted heavily from Jefferson's letter, noting with approbation Jefferson's view that the federal government was not to interfere with religious expressions or values, except in a very narrow category. After summarizing Jefferson's letter, the Court concluded:

> [T]he rightful purposes of civil government are for its officers to interfere [with religion only] when its principles break out into overt acts against peace and good order. In th[is] . . . is found the true distinction between what properly belongs to the Church and what to the State. . . . Congress was deprived of all legislative power over mere [religious] opinion, but was left free to reach [religious] actions which were in violation of social duties or subversive of good order. [40]

Since the federal government was only to inhibit religious expressions that were "subversive of good order" or "broke out into overt acts against peace and good order," that Court (and other courts, including in *Commonwealth v. Nesbit* [41] and *Lindenmuller v. The People* [42]) provided examples of the types of "religious" acts into which the government _did_ have legitimate reason to intrude – acts such as human sacrifice, concubinage, incest, polygamy, injury to children, etc. But in traditional religious practices (whether public prayer, the use of the Scriptures, etc.), the government was **_never_** to interfere. This was the clearly understood meaning of Jefferson's "separation" letter and the manner in which it was applied for a century-and-a-half.

However, a reversal occurred in 1947 in *Everson v. Board of Education*, [43] when the Supreme Court for the first time interpreted the "separation" phrase as requiring the federal government to *remove* religious expressions from the public arena – that is, it interpreted the First Amendment not as a limitation on government interference but rather as a limitation on religious expressions and principles. That Court, unlike previous ones, did not reprint Jefferson's letter (a very short letter) but cited only eight words from the letter ("a wall of separation between church and state"). Furthermore, the Court did not give the context of the phrase, or Jefferson's numerous other statements on the subject; in fact, it did not even mention that previous Supreme Courts had used Jefferson's letter to *preserve* religious principles in public society rather than remove them. In short, that 1947 Court was the first to divorce Jefferson's metaphor from its context and then apply it in a manner exactly opposite to Jefferson's clearly articulated intent.

Fifteen years after redefining Jefferson's phrase, in the 1962 decision *Engel v. Vitale*, [44] the Court began redefining individual words within that phrase. For example, the Court determined that "church" would no longer mean a federal denomination (as had been its meaning for the previous two centuries) but that "church" would now mean a public religious activity. Therefore, "separation of church and state" no longer meant that the federal government (i.e., the "state") could not establish a federal denomination (i.e., a "church"), but it now meant that public religious expressions (i.e., the new "church") must be kept separate from the public square (i.e., the new "state"). This change in definition has resulted in one absurd ruling after another.

For example, in *Stone v. Graham*, the Supreme Court ruled that because of the new "separation of church and state" it was unconstitutional for a student at school to continue, even *voluntarily*, to see a copy of the Ten Commandments. The Court explained:

> If the posted copies of the Ten Commandments are to have any effect at all, it will be to induce the schoolchildren to read, meditate upon, perhaps to venerate and obey the Commandments... [T]his ... is not a permissible ... objective. [45]

According to the Court, if students – even voluntarily – were to look at a copy of the Ten Commandments, they might respect and even obey teachings such as "do not steal" and "do not kill"; that would be unconstitutional. This bizarre logic is reflective of far too many of the Court's religion decisions handed down since 1962 – including its 1963 *Abington v. Schempp* [46] decision.

In that case, the Court reversed more than two centuries of precedent (including its own previous rulings [47]), ordering that the Bible and its teachings no longer be permitted in public education. Why? According to the Court:

> [I]f portions of the New Testament were read without explanation, they could be and ... had been psychologically harmful to the child [student]. [48]

What an amazing pronouncement: the Scriptures can cause psychological damage – that is, exposing students to Biblical teachings (such as the Golden Rule, the Beatitudes, and the Good Samaritan) can cause lasting brain damage!

The Founding Fathers had specifically forewarned of the adverse effects of excluding religious influences from the public arena. (Recall Declaration signer Benjamin Rush, Bill of Rights signer John Adams, and Speaker of the House Robert Winthrop had specifically warned that if the public teaching of the Bible were restricted, crime and violent behavior would escalate.) It is therefore not surprising that there have been measurable societal changes in the wake of the Court's rulings.

For example, following the Court's 1962-1963 decisions to exclude basic religious teachings from students, violent crime increased 700 percent, [49] with metal detectors and uniformed police officers becoming a normal part of the student educational experience. In fact, crime so exploded among junior high students that the federal government began separate tracking of murders, assaults, and rapes committed by students ages 10-14 (significantly, none of these categories of statistics existed before the Court's decisions – that is, these crimes occurred so infrequently that separate monitoring of these problems was unnecessary). Yet, despite these alarming trends and burgeoning increases in violent crime among students, they still cannot be permitted to see things such as "don't steal" or "don't kill" – or even teachings such as the Golden Rule or the Good Samaritan – for they might obey those teachings, and that would not only be unconstitutional but it also might cause them psychological harm!

The incongruity of this public policy became apparent to Colorado's State Board of Education following the frightful school shootings at Columbine. After serious introspection in the wake of that tragedy, the Board issued a letter openly acknowledging:

> As we seek the why behind this infamous event, we must find answers beyond the easy and obvious. How weapons become used for outlaw purposes is assuredly a relevant issue, yet our society's real problem is how human behavior sinks to utter and depraved indifference to the sanctity of life. As our country promotes academic literacy, we must promote moral literacy as well. . . . Our tragedy is but the latest – albeit the most terrifying and costly – of a steadily escalating series of schoolhouse horrors that have swept across the nation. The senseless brutality of these calamities clearly reveals that a dangerous subculture of amoral violence has taken hold among many of our youth. . . . . [W]e must remember, respect, and unashamedly take pride in the fact that our schools, like our country, found their origin and draw their strength from the faith-based morality that is at the heart of our national character. Today our schools have become so fearful of affirming one religion or one value over another that they have banished them all. In doing so they have abdicated their historic role in the moral formation of youth and thereby alienated themselves from our people's deep spiritual sensibilities. To leave this disconnection between society and its schools unaddressed is an open invitation to further divisiveness and decline. For the sake of our children, who are so dependent upon a consistent and unified message from the adult world,

we must solve these dilemmas. . . . Perhaps across the ages we can hear the timeless words of Abraham Lincoln, and, applying them to our own circumstance, renew his pledge "that we here highly resolve that these dead shall not have died in vain; that this nation, under God, shall have a new birth of freedom." With history as our judge, let us go forward together with a strong and active faith. [50]

The letter from the Colorado State Board of Education is simply recognizing the wisdom of the federal law signed by President George Washington on August 7, 1789, stipulating that schools and education systems were indeed the proper means to encourage the "religion, morality, and knowledge" so "necessary to good government and the happiness of mankind." [51]

Another aspect of behavior directly impacted by the removal of religious principles was morality. Recall that both George Washington and Fisher Ames had warned that neither national morality in general nor student morality in particular could be maintained apart from religious principles. Statistics now verify the accuracy of their warnings.

For example, following the 1962-1963 court-ordered removal of religious principles from students, teenage pregnancies immediately soared over 700 percent, [52] with the United States recording the highest teen pregnancy rates in the industrialized world. [53] Similarly, sexual activity among fifteen year-olds skyrocketed, [54] and sexually transmitted diseases among students ascended to previously unrecorded levels. [55] In fact, virtually every moral measurement kept by federal cabinet-level agencies reflects the same statistical pattern: the removal of religious principles from the public sphere was accompanied by a corresponding decline in public morality. [56]

To help combat the escalating teen pregnancy rates, some schools began to teach abstinence; but opponents of that teaching claimed that pre-marital sexual abstinence was a "religious" teaching and that it thus violated "separation of church and state." They therefore filed suit in court, where judges agreed with their view and disallowed the teaching of abstinence. [57] The sex education curriculum utilized by the opponents is described as "comprehensive sex-education" and takes an approach in which no morals – no "rights" or "wrongs" – are presented. Instead, students are told all the various possibilities of what can be done sexually in cultures around the world and then encouraged to make their own choices, no matter how extreme or abhorrent (or even illegal under American laws) those sexual behaviors may be. In essence, students are told: "It's your sexual life – live it as you choose! Do not let anyone tell you what is right or wrong. Do what is sexually pleasurable for you."

With such teachings, it certainly is not surprising that teen pregnancy rates soared – as did the massive economic costs associated with teen mothers. What economic costs? According to recent statistics, eighty percent of teen mothers end up on welfare; [58] half of all long-term welfare recipients started their families as teens; [59] and teen mothers are much more likely to live below the poverty level. [60] Consequently, over $9 billion dollars is spent annually through federal, state, and local welfare and poverty programs to address the economic costs of teen pregnancies. [61]

In an attempt to reduce the extremely high teen pregnancy rate and the massive governmental spending that it generates, Congress passed the Adolescent Family Life Act, offering federal grant money to any group that would teach pre-marital sexual abstinence. [62] Not surprisingly, that law, like the previous abstinence measures, was immediately challenged and taken to court, where the lower court held that abstinence was a religious teaching and thus could not be taught to students. [63] That ruling was appealed to the U. S. Supreme Court, where logic seems to be reasserting itself: the Court reversed the lower court decision and held that even though abstinence was a religious teaching, it was nevertheless beneficial for students. [64]

Following that ruling, nearly a dozen major "abstinence only" curriculums were placed in public schools [65] (a number that is still increasing); furthermore, nearly two-dozen states have now passed laws mandating "abstinence only" teachings in schools. [66] And just as the removal of religious moral teachings had a verifiable negative impact, so, too, did their reintroduction have a verifiable positive impact.

The reversal in teen pregnancy rates following the return of abstinence teaching is so marked that the teen pregnancy rate has reached its lowest point in three decades, [67] and current studies report:

> [A]mong unmarried teenage girls ages 15 to 19, increased abstinence accounted for 67 percent of the decrease in the pregnancy rate. Similarly, a 51 percent drop in the birth rate for single teenage girls ages 15 to 19 is attributed to abstinence. . . . These findings are significant because they refute the previous – and widely accepted – claims that the decrease in birth and pregnancy rates is due primarily to the increased use and effectiveness of contraception, such as condoms. [68]

Numerous other studies confirm similarly effective results, [69] demonstrating that the inclusion of basic religious principles does indeed produce morality and self-control, exactly as predicted by George Washington, Fisher Ames, and many other Framers.

Other indications of positive emerging judicial trends are seen in recent Supreme Court rulings that now make it permissible to have evangelism, prayer, and Bible clubs on public school campuses; [70] show films – in school facilities – that present family values from a religious perspective; [71] and pay for some student religious publications with school funds. [72] In fact, the Bible can even be taught as a for-credit course on public school campuses. [73]

In another promising trend, the Supreme Court now upholds the right of states and local communities to ban nude dancing. [74] (In recent years, courts have ruled that nude dancing was "free speech" or "free expression" and therefore could not be prohibited. [75]) The Court has now held that nude dancing *per se* is **not** speech but rather is behavior and therefore **can** be regulated. In fact, the Court cited statistics to prove that in communities with nude dancing, the crime rates and sexual assault rates were *higher* than in communities without nude dancing, explaining that nude dancing "encourages prostitution, increases sexual assaults, and attracts other criminal activity." [76] The Court therefore held that it was not only permissible but even desirable to uphold certain moral standards, even though many may consider those standards to be religious (the Court calls this the Secondary-Effects Doctrine).

In yet another positive change, there is now a renewed interest in teaching accurate history in schools, even when specific aspects of that history are overtly religious. Consequently, nearly a dozen state legislatures have passed laws encouraging teachers to post in classrooms the writings of the Founding Fathers and the documents from our history that have strong religious content, but which have largely disappeared from textbooks (e.g., the Mayflower Compact of 1620, the Northwest Ordinance of 1787, George Washington's "Farewell Address" of 1796, Lincoln's Second Inaugural Address of 1865, etc.). [77] These new laws prohibit content-based censorship of American history due to the religious references found in those documents.

In conclusion, historically speaking, the "separation of church and state" was never intended to become a tool to secularize the public square; to the contrary, the Founding Fathers intended that Biblical principles be part of public society and believed that the "separation" doctrine would preserve those principles in the public arena rather than prohibit them. And statistically speaking, the inclusion of Biblical principles and values in societal programs produces positive measurable results. Therefore, citizens should not be intimidated from utilizing those principles or values, not only because they were constitutionally protected and are now being slowly reaffirmed by the courts, but especially because they work! America will be morally and culturally strong only to the degree that Biblical, religious and moral principles are incorporated throughout society and its institutions, so take courage and stand up for what has been proven to be successful! ■

Endnotes

1. Abram E. Brown, *John Hancock: His Book* (Boston: Lee and Shepard Publishers, 1898), p. 269, Hancock's Inaugural Address as Governor of Massachusetts, 1780.

2. John Adams, *The Works of John Adams, Second President of the United States*, Charles Francis Adams, editor (Boston: Little, Brown and Company, 1850), Vol. IX, p. 229, "To the Officers of the First Brigade of the Third Division of the Militia of Massachusetts on October 11, 1798."

3. Benjamin Rush, *Essays, Literary, Moral, and Philosophical* (Philadelphia: Thomas & Samuel F. Bradford, 1798), p. 83.

4. Thomas Jefferson, *The Writings of Thomas Jefferson*, Albert Ellery Bergh, editor (Washington, DC: The Thomas Jefferson Memorial Association, 1904), Vol. XII, p. 315, to James Fishback, September 27, 1809.

5. Robert Treat Paine, *The Papers of Robert Treat Paine*, Stephen T. Riley and Edward W. Hanson, editors (Boston: Massachusetts Historical Society, 1992), Vol. I, p. 48, Robert Treat Paine's Confession of Faith, 1749.

6. Bernard C. Steiner, *The Life and Correspondence of James McHenry* (Cleveland: The Burrows Brothers Company, 1907), p. 475, from Charles Carroll, November 4, 1800.

7. John Witherspoon, *The Works of the Rev. John Witherspoon* (Philadelphia: William W. Woodard, 1802), Vol. III, pp. 41-42, 46, "The Dominion of Providence Over the Passions of Men," May 17, 1776.

8. George Washington, *Address of George Washington, President of the United States... Preparatory to his Declination* (Baltimore: George and Henry S. Keatinge, 1796), pp. 22-23.

9. Benjamin Franklin, *The Works of Benjamin Franklin*, Jared Sparks, editor (Boston: Tappan, Whittemore, and Mason, 1840), Vol. X, p. 282, to Thomas Paine in 1790.

10. Bernard C. Steiner, *One Hundred and Ten Years of Bible Society Work in Maryland* (Baltimore: Maryland Bible Society, 1921), p. 14.

11. Charles C. Jones, *Biographical Sketches of the Delegates from Georgia to the Continental Congress* (Boston: Houghton, Mifflin and Company, 1891), pp. 6-7.

12. Jared Sparks, *The Life of Gouverneur Morris* (Boston: Gray and Bowen, 1832), Vol. III, p. 483, "Notes on the Form of a Constitution for France."

13. *United States Oracle* (Portsmouth, NH), May 24, 1800; see also *The Documentary History of the Supreme Court of the United States, 1789-1800*, Maeva Marcus, editor (New York: Columbia University Press, 1988), Vol. III, p. 436.

14. Patrick Henry, *Life, Correspondence and Speeches*, William Wirt Henry, editor (New York: Charles Scribner's Sons, 1891), Vol. I, p. 82, handwritten endorsement on the back of the paper containing resolutions of the Virginia Assembly in 1765 concerning the Stamp Act.

15. Noah Webster, *History of the United States* (New Haven: Durrie & Peck, 1832), p. 339, ¶ 53.

16. John Quincy Adams, *Letters of John Quincy Adams to His Son on the Bible and its Teachings* (Auburn: James M. Alden, 1850), pp. 22-23.

17. Daniel Webster, *The Works of Daniel Webster* (Boston: Little, Brown, & Co., 1853), Vol. II, p. 615, "Address Delivered at the Laying of the Cornerstone of the Addition to

the Capitol," July 4, 1851; see also Vol. I, p. 44, "A Discourse Delivered at Plymouth on December 22, 1820."

18. John Marshall, *The Papers of John Marshall*, Charles Hobson, editor (Chapel Hill: University of North Carolina Press, 2006), Vol. XII, p. 278, to Rev. Jasper Adams on May 9, 1833.

19. John Adams, *Works*, Vol. X, p. 45, to Thomas Jefferson, June 28, 1813.

20. American Presidency Project, "Harry S. Truman: Address at the Lighting of the National Community Christmas Tree on the White House Grounds" (at http://www.presidency.ucsb.edu/ws/?pid=12569).

21. Alexis de Tocqueville, *Democracy in America* (London: Saunders and Otley, 1838), Vol. II, p. 144.

22. *Debates and Proceedings in the Congress of the United States* (Washington, DC: Gales & Seaton, 1834), Vol. I, pp. 439-951, June 8-September 24, 1789; and *Journal of the First Session of the Senate of the United States of America, Begun and Held at the City of New York, March 4, 1789* (Washington, DC: Gales & Seaton, 1820), pp. 69-88, September 2-25, 1798.

23. *Debates and Proceedings*, Vol. I, p. 451, June 8, 1789; see also Vol. I, pp. 757-759, August 15, 1789.

24. *Journal . . . of the Senate*, p. 70, September 3, 1789.

25. *Debates and Proceedings*, Vol. I, p. 796, August 20, 1789.

26. Fisher Ames, *Works of Fisher Ames* (Boston: T. B. Wait & Co., 1809), p. 134, January 1801.

27. Ames, *Works*, pp. 134-135.

28. *Dictionary of American Biography*, s.v. "Benjamin Rush"; see also Rush, *Essays*, p. 1, "A Plan for Establishing Public Schools in Pennsylvania and for Conducting Education Agreeably to a Republican form of Government."

29. Rush, *Essays*, p. 112, "A Defense of the Use of the Bible as a School Book."

30. Webster, *History*, p. 339, ¶ 53.

31. John Adams, *Works*, Vol. IX, p. 229, "To the Officers of the First Brigade of the Third Division of the Militia of Massachusetts on October 11, 1798."

32. Robert Winthrop, *Addresses and Speeches on Various Occasions* (Boston: Little, Brown, and Company, 1852), p. 172, "An Address Delivered at the Annual Meeting of the Massachusetts Bible Society in Boston," May 28, 1849.

33. Washington, *Address*, pp. 22-23.

34. Washington, *Address*, p. 23.

35. Washington, *Address*, p. 23.

36. Letter of October 7, 1801 from Danbury (CT) Baptist Association to Thomas Jefferson, from the Thomas Jefferson Papers, Manuscript Division, Library of Congress, Washington, DC.

37. Jefferson, *Writings*, Vol. XVI, pp. 281-282, to the Danbury Baptist Association, January 1, 1802.

38. Jefferson, *Writings*, Vol. XVI, pp. 281-282, to the Danbury Baptist Association, January 1, 1802.

39. *The Jeffersonian Cyclopedia*, John P. Foley, editor (New York: Funk & Wagnalls, 1900), p. 977; see also *Documents of American History*, Henry S. Commager, editor (New York: Appleton-Century-Crofts, Inc., 1948), p. 179; *Annals of the Congress of the United States* (Washington, DC: Gales and Seaton, 1852), Eighth Congress, Second Session, p. 78,

March 4, 1805; see also James D. Richardson, *A Compilation of the Messages and Papers of the Presidents*, 1789-1897 (Published by Authority of Congress, 1899), Vol. I, p. 379, March 4, 1805; Jefferson, *Writings*, Vol. XVI, p. 325, to the Society of the Methodist Episcopal Church on December 9, 1808; Thomas Jefferson, *Memoir, Correspondence, and Miscellanies, From the Papers of Thomas Jefferson*, Thomas Jefferson Randolph, editor (Boston: Gray and Bowen, 1830), Vol. IV, pp. 103-104, to the Rev. Samuel Miller, January 23, 1808.

40. *Reynolds v. U. S.*, 98 U.S. 145, 163-164 (1878).

41. *Commonwealth v. Nesbit*, 84 Pa. 398 (Sup. Ct. Penn. 1859).

42. *Lindenmuller v. The People*, 33 Barb 548 (Sup. Ct. NY 1861).

43. *Everson v. Board of Education*, 330 U.S. 1, 18 (1947).

44. *Engel v. Vitale*, 370 U.S. 421 (1962).

45. *Stone v. Graham*, 449 U.S. 39, 42 (1980).

46. *Abington v. Schempp*, 374 U.S. 203 (1963).

47. *Vidal v. Girard's Executors*, 43 U.S. 127 (1844).

48. *Abington* at 209.

49. David Barton, *America: To Pray or Not To Pray?* (Aledo, TX: WallBuilder Press, 1994), p. 88, data from the *Statistical Abstracts of the United States*, and the Department of Commerce, Census Bureau.

50. Colorado State Board of Education, "What Is To Be Done: Searching for Meaning in Our Tragedy" (at http://www.cde.state.co.us/cdeboard/bdcolumbine.htm).

51. *The Constitutions of the United States of America With the Latest Amendments* (Trenton: Moore and Lake, 1813), p. 364, "An Ordinance of the Territory of the United States Northwest of the River Ohio," Article III.

52. Barton, *To Pray*, pp. 27-28, data obtained from the Department of Health and Human Services; the Center for Disease Control; *Statistical Abstracts of the United States*; and the Department of Commerce, Census Bureau.

53. National Campaign to Prevent Teen Pregnancy, "By the Numbers: The Public Costs of Teen Childbearing" (at http://www.teenpregnancy.org/costs/pdf/report/BTN_National_Report.pdf).

54. Alan Guttmacher Institute, *Family Planning Perspectives*, Vol. 19, No. 2, March/April 1987.

55. Barton, *To Pray*, pp. 30-31, data obtained from the Department of Health and Human Services and the Center for Disease Control.

56. Barton, *To Pray*, pp. 26, 31, 33, 51-53, 88, 98-104, data obtained from Department of Health and Human Services; the *Statistical Abstracts of the United States*; The Center for Disease Control; *Family Planning Perspectives*, March/April 1987; *Sexual and Reproductive Behavior of American Women*, 1982-88, furnished by the Alan Guttmacher Institute; U.S. National Center for Health Statistics, *Vital Statistics of the United States*, annual; Department of Commerce, Census Bureau; *National Study on Child Neglect and Abuse Reporting*, annual, provided by American Humane Association, Denver, CO; *AIDS Weekly Surveillance Report – United States*, Center for Disease Control; *National Survey of Drug Abuse*, provided by National Institute on Drug Abuse; University of Michigan Survey, *Reader's Digest*, August 1983, p. 138; and many, many other post-1963 governmental sources.

57. See, for example, *Kendrick v. Bowen*, 657 F. Supp. 1547 (D.D.C. 1987); see also *ACLU of Louisiana v. Foster*, No. 02-1440 (2002).

58. Brookings Institute, "What Can Be Done to Reduce Teen Pregnancy and Out-of-Wedlock Births?" (at www.brookings.edu/es/research/projects/wrb/publications/pb/pb08.htm).

59. Brookings Institute, "What Can Be Done to Reduce Teen Pregnancy and Out-of-Wedlock Births?" (at www.brookings.edu/es/research/projects/wrb/publications/pb/pb08.htm).

60. Brookings Institute, "What Can Be Done to Reduce Teen Pregnancy and Out-of-Wedlock Births?" (at www.brookings.edu/es/research/projects/wrb/publications/pb/pb08.htm).

61. National Campaign to Prevent Teen Pregnancy, "By the Numbers: The Public Costs of Teen Childbearing" (at www.teenpregnancy.org/costs/pdf/report/BTN_National_Report.pdf).

62. Adolescent Family Life Demonstration Projects, *U.S. Code*, Vol. 42, Sections 300z-2-300z-3 (1981).

63. *Kendrick v. Bowen*, 657 F. Supp. 1547 (1987).

64. *Bowen v. Kendrick*, 487 U.S. 589 (1988).

65. Dinah Richard, *Has Sex Education Failed Our Teenagers?* (Colorado Springs: Focus on the Family Publishing, 1990), p. 85.

66. SEICUS, "Policy and Advocacy" (at http://www.siecus.org/policy/states/2005/select-Topics.html).

67. See, for example, Guttmacher Institute, "U.S. Teenage Pregnancy Statistics National and State Trends and Trends by Race and Ethnicity" (at http://www.guttmacher.org/pubs/2006/09/12/USTPstats.pdf).

68. *Adolescent and Family Health Journal*, April 2003, cited in Heritage Foundation, "Increased Abstinence Causes a Large Drop in Teen Pregnancy" (at http://www.heritage.org/Research/Abstinence/em872.cfm).

69. See, for example, Heritage Foundation, "More Evidence of the Effectiveness of Abstinence Education" (at http://www.heritage.org/Research/Abstinence/wm738.cfm) and "The Effectiveness of Abstinence Education Programs in Reducing Sexual Activity Among Youth" (at http://www.heritage.org/Research/Abstinence/BG1533.cfm).

70. *Westside v. Mergens*, 496 U.S. 226 (1990); and *Good News Club v. Milford*, 121 S. Ct. 2093 (2001).

71. *Lamb's Chapel v. Center Moriches Union Free Sch. Dist.*, 508 U.S. 384 (1993).

72. *Rosenberger v. Rector and Visitors of Univ. of Va.*, 515 U.S. 819 (1995).

73. For information on such curriculum and its use, contact the National Council on Bible Curriculum in Public Schools, Elizabeth Ridenour, PO Box 9743, Greensboro, NC 27429, 336-272-3799, www.bibleinschools.net.

74. *Barnes v. Glen*, 115 L. Ed. 2d. 504 (1991); and *City of Erie, et al. v. Pap's A. M. tdba "KANDYLAND,"* 529 U.S. 277 (2000).

75. See, for example, *In re Giannini*, 69 Cal. 2d 563, 446 P.2d 535 (1968); *Salem Inn, Inc. v. Frank*, 501 F.2d 18 (2dCir.1974); *Salem Inn, Inc. v. Frank*, 522 F.2d 1045 (2dCir.1975); *Kuzinich v. County of Santa Clara*, 689 F.2d 1345 (9thCir.1982); *Krueger v. City of Pensacola*, 759 F.2d 851, 854 (11thCir.1985); *International Food & Beverage System v. Fort Lauderdale*, 794 F.2d 1520, 1525 (11thCir.1986); *Kev, Inc. v. Kitsap County*, 793 F.2d 1053, 1058 (9thCir.1986); *BSA, Inc. v. King County*, 804 F.2d 1104, 1107 (9thCir.1986); *Walker v. City of Kansas City, Mo.*, 691 F.Supp. 1243, 1249 (W.D.Mo.1988); *Doe v. City of Minneapolis*, 693

F.Supp. 774, 779 n. 12 (D.Minn.1988); *LLEH, Inc. v. Wichita County, Texas*, 121 F. Supp. 2d 513 (N.D. Tex. 2000); *Pap's A.M. v. City of Erie*, 812 A.2d 591 (Pa. 2002) (Pap's III); *Bosley v. WildWetT.com*, 70 U.S.P.Q.2d 1537, 2004 WL 2169179 (6th Cir. 2004); *Conchatta Inc. v. Miller*, F.3d ---, 2006 WL 2347649 (3d Cir. Aug. 15, 2006); *Missouri Association of Club Executives v. State of Missouri*, SC87154 (Mo. 2006), *City of Daytona Beach, Florida v. Elizabeth M. Book*, No. 20050021caap (7th Fla. Cir. Ct. Nov. 2, 2006); etc.

76. *Barnes v. Glen*, 115 L. Ed. 2d. 504, 522 (1991).

77. See, for example, the Kentucky Revised Statutes, §158.195; Arizona Revised Statutes, §15-717; Tennessee Code Annotated, §49-6-1011; West Virginia Code §18-5-41; Arkansas Code, §6-16-122; Indiana Code, §20-10.1-4-2.5; Louisiana (§RS 17:2117, and §RS 25:1281-1284); Utah (§53A-13-101.4); Minnesota (§120B.235); Mississippi (§37-13-163); North Carolina (§115C-81(g)); etc.

Also Available from WallBuilders

A history curriculum that unabashedly delivers the truth!
Drive Through History America
written by David Barton & presented by award-winning actor Dave Stotts

Visit our website for other great resources!

800-873-2845 • www.wallbuilders.com